CROMFORD &
HIGH PEAK RAIL[WAY]
Picture Album

Tony Broome

Willow Publishing 1985
Willow Cottage, 36 Moss Lane,
Timperley, Altrincham,
Cheshire, WA15 6SZ.

ISBN 0 946361 01 0

Printed by The Commercial
Centre Ltd., Clowes Street,
Hollinwood, Oldham.

opposite page:
A North London Tank approaching
the top of Hopton Incline with a quite
exceptional train of 2 water tanks and
seven loaded wagons, the last two
containing great blocks of limestone.

Introduction

In April 1967 I received an invitation from a member of the Derbyshire County Council, who were considering buying the track, for a ride on the last-but-one train on the Cromford and High Peak Railway from Middleton Top to Parsley Hay and back. Until that moment I had never given the "High Peak Railway", as it was known locally, a second glance. I realised I was watching the end of an era which had lasted from 1830 until 1967 and resolved to photograph everything which remained. This I did, not just the engines but the men who worked the railway, the buildings, the track, bridges, signals, notices and so on – in fact everything.

Eventually the collection grew to over 400 pictures. Some were purchased from commercial undertakings but the great majority were from amateur photographers and, especially, from the family albums of the men who worked the railway. Many of these latter worked through three generations and an astonishing number of pictures from the 1880's and maybe ealier have turned up in remote Peakland cottage photo albums. They represent a unique record of a unique railway.

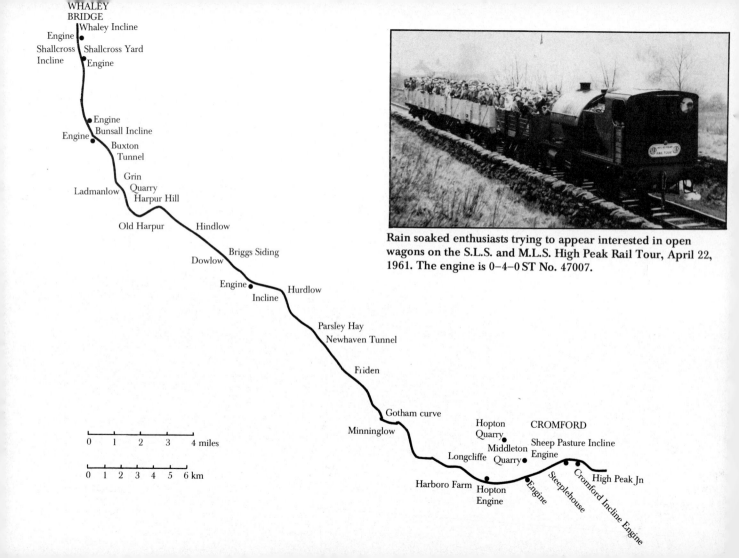

WHALEY BRIDGE
Whaley Incline
Engine
Shallcross Incline
Shallcross Yard
Engine
Engine
Bunsall Incline
Engine
Buxton Tunnel
Grin Quarry
Ladmanlow
Harpur Hill
Old Harpur
Hindlow
Briggs Siding
Dowlow
Engine
Incline
Hurdlow
Parsley Hay
Newhaven Tunnel
Friden
Gotham curve
Minninglow
Hopton Quarry
CROMFORD
Middleton Quarry
Sheep Pasture Incline
Engine
Longcliffe
Harboro Farm
Hopton Engine
Engine
Steeplehouse
Cromford Incline Engine
High Peak Jn

0 1 2 3 4 miles
0 1 2 3 4 5 6 km

Rain soaked enthusiasts trying to appear interested in open wagons on the S.L.S. and M.L.S. High Peak Rail Tour, April 22, 1961. The engine is 0-4-0 ST No. 47007.

Driver Joe Gould on a Webb 0–4–2 Tank "Bissel Truck" carefully propelling a wagon to the foot of Sheep Pasture Incline in 1932. The Engine is L.M.S. No. 7861 and was formerly L.N.W.R. No. 3525. Behind the engine rakes of wagons and water tanks are standing on the sidings of Cromford Wharf. It is just possible to discern the chimney of the pumping engine, still in good running order, which was used to pump water from the River Derwent into the Cromford Canal.

View up Sheep Pasture incline from the main A6 road bridge showing the catch-pit and pointsman's cabin, track and ropes.

The transit shed and warehouse at Cromford Wharf, looking towards Sheep Pasture. The old banner signal is clearly showing "Danger" to the line.

The interior of the workshop at Cromford about 1880. Upon closure of the Cromford end of the line in 1967 this building was made secure against vandals by the new owners, Derbyshire County Council, and 15 years later very little has changed. To enter the workshop is to step back 100 years in time. The fish bellied rails secured to stone blocks survive, as does the forge, the old tools and a cylinder from one of the winding engines.

In the photograph, the man second from the left with the wooden right leg was William Hallows who worked on the High Peak Railway from September 1856 to March 1904.

above left:
Cromford joiner Vic Edge on the special British Ropes Wagon installing a new winding rope at the foot of Sheep Pasture Incline. The rope when spliced together had a continuous length of 2,880 yards.

above right:
A water tank wagon on the frame of a tender from one of McConnell's engines, probably dating from the late 1840's.

At one time there were 21 old tenders in use, filled from a large cistern which was fed from a spring opposite the workshop at Cromford and delivered at various points along the railway to supply stationary engines, locomotives and cottages.

right:
George Slack, Tommy Webber and Herbert Gillott by the Cromford Canal, just outside the Transit Shed.

Three wagons in the Sheep Pasture Incline catch-pit some time before 1920. One of the wagons has been broken in half by the impact and the broken winding rope can be seen coiled up in the foreground. Beside the catch-pit is milepost no.23. This was probably the 4 March 1903 runaway, as a roof was later installed over the pit and damaged on 20 May 1916 when five wagons ran 1120 yards down the incline and into the pit with great violence.

Cromford Wharf with the water tanks on the left and the workshops. The engine is an old Caledonian Railway 0–4–0 saddle tank, most probably No. 56020 which was kept at Burton-on-Trent at the time. Burton engines were occasionally sent to Cromford to help out when the regular locos were sick.

0–4–2 Saddle Tank, L.M.S. No. 7859 at Cromford Shed, 29 August, 1935, with the canal in the foreground. This engine was previously numbered 6409, ex-L.N.W.R. No. 3473. This building was unfortunately demolished after the line closed and no trace remains.

Locomotive foreman Merrill and traffic inspector Jack Smith standing proudly by the banner signal at Cromford Wharf. Behind is the terrace of railwaymen's houses known as "Railway End".

An Allan 'Crewe Goods' 2–4–0 Tank at Cromford Wharf about 1890. The engine is L.M.W.R. No. 3097 and started life as a tender engine. It was the last-but-one survivor of a once numerous class. In the right background can be seen a signal on the Midland Railway with the old horizontal black stripe on the back.

In January 1903 this engine was sold to Fenton Colliery, Alsager.

above:

Cromford Incline. One of the treadles depressed by the wheels of passing wagons descending the incline. The treadles were connected by wires to gongs and the pointsman at the catch-pit was thereby able to estimate the speed of descending traffic.

left:

A "hanger on" unroping a run of wagons at the foot of Sheep Pasture Incline.

The foot of the Cromford Incline, 15 April, 1934. Past cleaner Sam Buckley and bicycle are about to travel home to Middleton on an ascending water tank. 33 years and 16 days later, driver Buckley took the last train from Middleton Top to Friden when that section of the line finally closed. Carefully ignoring him in front of the telephone box are a visitor, shunter Tom Beeson and wagon examiner Jack Oldbury.

BACK ROW (standing) left to right: Jack Oldbury, *Wagon Examiner,* known as "Tapper Jack" from his practice of tapping wagon wheels with a hammer; Tom Swift, *Guard;* Harold Kirk, *Fireman,* William Boden, *Driver,* "Billy Boden" who died in the Hopton derailment; Jack Harrison, *Fireman;* Bernard Walker, *Fireman;* unidentified; Joe Nadin, *Hanger-on;* David Bond, *Winding Engineman at Sheep Pasture;* Luther Gould, "He was the *Goods Agent* at Crawford, he had his own office and several men working for him."

MIDDLE ROW (sitting) left to right: Herbert Hallowes, *Winding Engineman at Middleton,* father of Herbert Hallowes who appears in later pictures and was also a Winding Engineman; Herbert Slack, *Guard,* at Middleton; Len Spencer, still alive last summer; Tom Webber, *Number taker,* died this year; Herbert Evans, *Pointsman at Catchpit,* on Sheep Pasture; Dick Doxey, *Hanger-on,* Middleton Top; – Farnsworth, *Chief Clerk* in Luther Gould's Office, Christian name forgotten.

FRONT ROW (kneeling) left to right: Tom Huddert, *Blacksmith* at Crawford, known as "Tosser" from his football prowess. He ran the First Aid Classes of which this photograph depicts all the members in front of the Goods Shed at Steeple House, 1913. Billie Lamb, *Horse-dray Driver,* delivered goods locally by dray, worked for Luther Gould; Herbert Spencer, *Storekeeper,* worked in Luther Gould's office. Brother of Leonard. Appears in many later photographs; J. W. Spencer, *Plate-layer,* no relation!

The pointsman above the catch-pit on Sheep Pasture Incline preparing to divert a run of wagons around the pit, sometime before 1900. On the front of his cabin can be seen the gong operated by the flanges of the wheels of descending wagons.

The boiler of an old Ramsbottom DX class goods engine which was installed in Sheep Pasture Top winding engine house in 1884 after the original stationary winding engine wore out.

above:
Preparations to recover Kitson 0–4–0 Saddle Tank Engine No. 47000 from the garden of Station House, Steeple Grange, Wirksworth. After platelayers had left the points switched to the siding at Steeplehouse on the 29 July 1955, the crew of the first train next day inadvertently entered the siding instead of proceeding along the "main line". The engine was recovered by a caterpillar tractor along a temporary track and repaired at Derby Works.

This is a view of Steeplehouse about 1960. A Kitson 0–4–0 ST engine has brought a train of eight laden wagons of limestone cautiously down the 1 in 27 gradient of Killer's Branch from Middleton Quarry, visible top right, and is proceeding to Sheep Pasture Top. The building with a white roof (only reflected sunlight), centre left, is the old goods shed at Steeplehouse and the chimney of Middleton Top engine house can clearly be seen on the sky-line.

Fireman Harold Kirk (by the cab steps), cleaner Harry Hallows and driver Elijah Sheldon on L.N.W.R. 2–4–0 Tank No. 2244. No doubt they are all very proud of their engine which shines like a mirror in the very best 19th century tradition, even in 1921. Posed outside Sheep Pasture Shed.

Driver Frank Brown with his immaculately turned-out No. 6422, formerly L.N.W.R. 2–4–0 T No. 2240. The picture is a good likeness of both driver and engine but unfortunately does not show the bottles of beer which "Hellfire Frank" invariably stowed away in his cab.

Sheep Pasture Top, August, 1966. The 204 h.p. Diesel No. D2383
which had arrived for the first time the previous day is standing
over the pit to the right of Kitson 0–4–0 Saddle Tank No. 47000,
whose duties it is about to take over.

The last of the North Western 'Choppers', L.M.S. 2–4–0 Tank No.
6428, simmering gently in the sunshine by the water tower at
Sheep Pasture Top during the summer of 1942.

Railway officers on an inspection tour slumming it somewhat in 1951. The limestone wall behind was built across the top of the Midland Railway's branch from Wirksworth which was never connected.

The white cross on the old tender indicated that it was not in revenue-earning service.

0-4-0 ST, B.R. No. 47000, crossing the Wirksworth to Middleton road with a train of limestone for Cromford. May 12, 1966.

Killer's Middleon Quarry, about 1920. The cut stone and rubble is being shifted solely by rail, mostly in Midland and L.N.W.R. wagons.

right:
Deeley Midland 0–4–0 T, B.R. No. 41536, at Steeplehouse. The engine has just crossed the bridge over the Cromford to Wirksworth road and the Killer's Branch can be seen diverging to the left near the wall. The right-hand line is the Steeplehouse Station siding. This engine was formerly M.R. and L.M.S. No. 1536.

left:

The Middleton end of Killer's Branch from the top of the quarry face, August 10, 1927. In the centre stands the stone-sawing and masonry works with a wagon of stone in the entrance. To the right of the works wagons are standing on the private siding, and to the right of this siding leads to the waste tip. Farther right still the Killer's Branch descends to Steeplehouse.

below left:

Kitson Saddle Tank, B.R. No. 47000, entering the vast limestone quarry of the Derbyshire stone firms at the end of the "Killer's Branch" and shunting in the Middleton quarry, 12 May, 1966.

below:

A little known feature of Cromford and High Peak operation. Tom Beeson is passing a kettle up to inspector Jack Smith to be filled from the water tank. Note the tender has a curved front end.

Kitson 0–4–0 Saddle Tank, B.R. No. 47000, descending Middleton Incline in steam with the counterbalancing water tank coming up. The line itself descends beneath a stone bridge carrying what was once the Middleton to Wirksworth road until it was quarried away.

The crews in later years always preferred to take the engines up and down Middleton incline rather than the much longer Sheep Pasture with its record of rope breakages and runaways.

A rake of wagons standing at the entrance to Middle Peak siding and coal yard, May 4, 1934. The quarry served by this siding at the turn of the century is visible in the background and Middleton Incline climbs through the trees up to the right.

J94 Tank, B.R. No. 68012, leaving Middleton Top in a cloud of steam with the last scheduled train from Middleton Top to Friden and Parsley Hay. To the left of the wooden fence is the long-disused and highly ruinous Stanton Ironworks Company's loading dock, and behind are two stone walls between which a tramway once ran from Middleton down to the line. 21 April, 1967.

Platelayers aligning the track at the foot of Hopton Incline. A wagon is standing on the siding to Magnesium Electron Ltd's works which closed on 20 June 1966 and were built on the site of the old Hopton Bone Manure Works.

Cylinder head, rod and beam motion right-hand side of the engine inside Middleton Top engine house.

The parallelogram linkage between beam and piston rod was devised by the great James Watt and he always claimed it was the invention of which he was most proud.

Indicator gear at Middleton Bottom for the planesman to signal to the engineman at the top of the incline, "B" indicated "Stand by" and "G" was "Go".

The loco shed and engineman's house at Middleton Top, June 5, 1950, with a North London tank basking in the sunshine. The engine is British Railways No. 58860 and was previously L.M.S. Nos. 7527 and 27527, L.N.W.R. No. 2892 and N.L.R. No. 92.

left:
Longcliffe Station group.
below left:
Middleton Top inside indicators, 13 June, 1951.
below:
Middleton Top outside indicators, 13 June, 1951.
Letters indicate "Stand by, Go and Stop"
respectively.

This photograph was taken at Middleton Top about 1880.
The engine is an Allan 'Crewe Goods' 2–4–0 Engine converted to
a tank engine. The driver and his fireman are standing on the
footplate. The man on the front framing has a special long oilcan
used to fill the lubricators on the valve gear which was rather
inaccessible between the main frames.

    Left to right the men standing appear to be:– foreman,

labourer, shunter with his pole, labourer, platelayer with shovel,
platelayer with pick, labourer, foreman, labourer, platelayer with
special hammer for knocking the wooden "keys" into the "chains"
of the track, another platelayer with hammer, foreman, platelayer
with special drill for making holes in sleepers to secure the chains
to the sleepers.

The stationary boiler for the winding engine behind the running shed at Middleton Top. The boiler was from an old (unidentified) goods engine which had been withdrawn for scrapping. It was cut up on the site in March, 1967.

Driver Sam Buckley in the cab of a J94 Tank Engine. Sam spent his whole working life on the "High Peak Railway", rising from cleaner, then fireman to driver and he took the very last scheduled train from Middleton to Parsley Hay on April 21 1967.

Middleton Top, September 30, 1961, with the winding house, black corrugated iron engine shed, elevated water tank and the elegant traffic inspector's office. Two J94 Saddle Tanks are standing at the head of a deserted Rail Tour train. Redhill siding diverges to the left just before the second brake van.

The wreckage of the 8.35 a.m. train from Middleton Top to Parsley Hay lying in the roadway at the foot of Hopton Incline. The locomotive was L.M.S. No. 27521, October 6, 1937. Driver Boden died in the accident which was caused by the engine spreading the track as a result of excessive speed. At the inquest the engine was stated to be in good condition at the time of the accident, having run 17,427 miles since its last overhaul in 1935. Fireman Harold Kirk, however, said it was the worst of the lot and he did not like it at all. It rode roughly, surged sideways and went round curves in a series of lurches. The track had been relaid in 1935 with L.N.W.R. material recovered from the main line. The weight of the 30′ rails, originally 90 lb. was then about 81 lb. per yard. The track was ballasted with ash, which was lacking in lateral stability.

A North London 0–6–0 Tank, L.M.S. No. 7527, emerging from Hoptonwood Quarries Branch, May 4, 1934. The course of the Branch can be seen descending to the left, the 113 yard Hopton tunnel is in the right distance and fireman Harold Kirk is on the footplate of old L. & N.W. No. 2892, ex-N.L.R. No. 92.

North London 0–6–0 Tank, L.M.S. No. 27530, at the foot of Hopton Incline, October 12, 1940. The names on the signpost have been removed as a wartime security measure. On this side of the bridge a stone carries the inscription: Emma Matilda Wilmot laid this stone may XVIII MDCCCXVII, and on the other side: Emma Thornhill laid this stone May XVIII MDCCCXVIII. The engine was L. & N.W. No. 2895, old North London No. 95.

Railwaymen's cottages at Hopton Top, 1968.

below:
Hopton Top, May 4, 1934. The mound on the left is the remains of the Hopton engine winding house, long since demolished.

Stephenson Locomotive Society and Manchester Locomotive
Society members observing driver Sam Buckley and fireman
Dennis Vallance performing the Cromford and High Peak ritual
of taking water for the engine from a pair of water tank wagons
on the elevated siding at Longcliffe.

Italian ex-prisoners-of-war helping railwaymen to clear the snows
of 1947 from Manystones cutting.

Old stone sleeper blocks used as steps, Longcliffe platform.

North London Tank, B.R. No. 58662, crossing the Grangemill to Ashbourne road at Longcliffe. This engine was L.M.S. No. 27530, was built in 1901, and retains its North London chimney. Longcliffe bridge is a fine early example of the use of cast iron in railway engineering. With a 19′ span it was built for Jessop by the Butterly Company in 1825. This bridge is a replacement of the original and was constructed by Smedley Bros. of Belper in 1865 at a cost of £5−15s. per ton for 26 tons of ironwork.

THIS STOP BOARD INDICATES
THE TERMINATION OF THE HOPTON
TOP TO LONGCLIFFE SECTION.
NO TRAIN OR ENGINE MUST
PASS THIS BOARD UNTIL
PERMISSION HAS BEEN OBTAINED
FROM THE STATION MASTER R
PERSON IN CHARGE AT LONGCLIFFE

The morning train from Middleton to Friden halted at the stop board marking the termination of the Hopton Top to Longcliffe section while permission is obtained to proceed into the Longcliffe. to Friden section. The guard's van is a London and North Western goods brake of about 1920.

S.L.S. and M.L.S. enthusiasts busily photographing J94 0–6–0 Tank No. 68006 in the sunshine at the head of an excursion at Longcliffe. The stationmaster's house with the stable doors at the end appears to be in a much better state of repair than it was 60 or 70 years earlier.

A family group at Station House, Longcliffe, about 1890. The portly flat-capped figure appears to be the stationmaster and a youth in railwayman's uniform is resting his elbows on the railway company's fence. The small boy in the centre is young Leonard Cope who was himself the stationmaster at Longcliffe for over 30 years, retiring in the early 1950's. Surprisingly the house looks very shabby especially when compared with photographs taken 60 or 70 years later. The end of the house contains a stables and hay loft possibly connected with the early use of horse traction on the line.

Approaching Longcliffe from Friden, taken from one of the brake vans of the R.C.T.S. Excursion, August 29, 1964. The train is crossing the Grangemill to Ashbourne road on the old Butterly bridge dating from the original opening of the line. Three vans are standing on the former milk-loading siding, just before which are the remains of a wooden turn-on scotch.

right:
Leonard Cope, station master at Longcliffe, with the yard staff, sometime about 1930.

Locomotive and staff in snow at Manystones cutting. This is probably the very severe winter of 1919 when drifts of 5 ft to 8 ft brought chaos for several days.

J94 0–6–0 Tank No.68012 on Minninglow Embankment, June 20th, 1966. The two water tanks are based on old Midland Railway tenders.

The R.C.T.S. Excursion, June 26, 1964. Train crossing the Via Gellia line to Newhaven Road behind a pair of J94 0–6–0 saddle tank engines. The crossing-keeper's cottage, the roof of which is just visible through the steam, was demolished about 1970 and no trace remains now.

J94 0–6–0 Tank No. 68012 on the penultimate Middleton Top to Parsley Hay working 19–4–67

An Allan 'Crewe Goods' 2–4–0 Engine, possibly L.N.W.R. No. 308, about 1870, halted on Gotham Curve with a train of 14 wagons, mostly of the Midland Railway. It is in unlined black with the number painted in yellow on the cabside and has lost its former name of "Booth". In other words it has almost been written off but not quite. The engine demonstrates admirably the 19th century opinion that fresh air and plenty of it was good for the enginemen. It kept them alert and stopped them from going to sleep on the job. The brake van appears to be the "Fly" in which passengers were carried in some discomfort on benches in the leading compartment. Passengers were carried from 1855 until the privilege was withdrawn in late 1877 following the fatal accident involving a traveller who was believed to have been a Minninglow rag-and-bone man.

Gotham Curve, 1932. This was the most severe curve on the main line with a radius of 55 yards and, at this time, a superelevation of 10⅛ inches.

Diesel 350 h.p. on test on Gotham Curve, 7 April, 1959. Worried railway staff are undecided whether the engine is straightening out Gotham Curve, or whether the track is bending the engine into a banana-shape. The loco, No. 12006, later disgraced itself by almost failing to climb Hopton Incline on its own, without the disadvantage of a train behind it!

North London Tank, B.R. No. 58856, dragging a creaking train of wagons laboriously round Gotham Curve in the direction of Longcliffe and Middleton – a view taken from the brake van.

When taking very long trains the crews would divide the train at the preceding loop and approach the curve with the engine in the middle. After pushing the front part round they would set back smartly for the rear half and on a good day they would catch up the front half while it was still rolling.

The S.L.S. and M.L.S. High Peak Railtour, April 22, 1961. The train is at Minninglow Station behind J94 0–6–0 ST, B.R. No. 68013. The siding was originally installed to serve the Minninglow Brickwords, of which few traces remain, and was used in later years for agricultural traffic.

North London Tank, B.R. No. 58860, setting back from Friden for Middleton, June 5, 1950. An L.N.W.R. brake van of about 1920 is at the rear of the train which No. 58860 has just brought from Middleton and which a class 3f 0–6–0 is about to take forward to Parsley Hay. Behind the sidings can be seen the chimneys of the Silica Firebrick works built on the site of the old Friden Station.

An officers inspection party at Friden, 1953. The carriage from which they have just emerged is an aged Midland Railway invalids saloon, converted to an officers saloon about 1947. The group includes R. J. Powell, district operating superintendent, Derby; T. F. Simpson, loco works manager and J. Knopman, district motive power superintendent, Longsight.

L.M.S. Class 2P 4–4–0 with an L.M.S. Open Brake 3rd carrying an official inspection party from Manchester at Friden, June 13, 1951. The driver has halted at the board indicating the end of the Parsley Hay to Friden section and is awaiting permission to proceed into the Friden to Longcliffe section.

J94 0–6–0 Saddle Tank, B.R. No. 68030, about to leave Friden for Middleton. This engine and No. 68013 were the first two war department engines to work this section of the line. The guard is holding the Friden to Longcliffe staff in his right hand.

below:
Two 3-car sets of diesel multiple unit stock approaching
Newhaven tunnel from the north, 3 May, 1959.

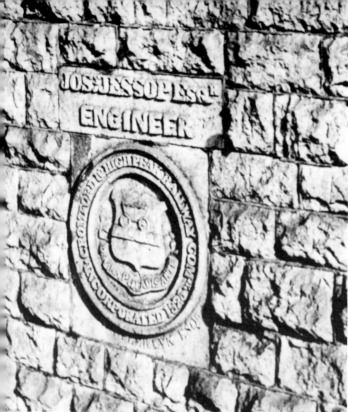

above:
The inscribed stone on the north face of Newhaven tunnel
showing the crest of C. & H.P.R., a 4-wheeled wagon on a shield,
with the motto "Davina Palladis Arte", the whole surrounded by a
garter reading "Cromford & High Peak Railway Comp'y
Incorporated 1825". Above is Jos. Jessop Esq. engineer and below
W. Brittlebank Esq.. Brittlebank & Son of Oddo House,
Wirksworth, were clerks to the company.

Parsley Hay Station, looking towards Hindlow, July 9, 1932. The double track reconstruction, opened on June 1, 1894, curves away to the left while the 1830 alignment on which an L.N.W.R. 0-8-0 is standing passed around the goods yard, right.

12006 and 2 petrol permanent way trolleys in Parsley Hay Station.

L.M.S. 4F 0–6–0 No. 3925 in Deep Valley Cutting, between Parsley Hay and Hurdlow. The snowdrift was 25 feet high and 600 feet long. March 23, 1947.

The L.N.W.R. two armed double faced signal at Ladmanlow, May 10, 1950. This was known as the Grin Branch Jct.. Signal post, and the upper arm was observed by drivers approaching from Friden. The lower arm was provided for Buxton Lime Co's engines going into and coming out of the Grin Branch. It was dismantled on June 7, 1950.

L.N.W.R. 'Crewe Goods' 2–4–0 No.308 at Hurdlow Top some
time between about 1870 and 1890. The figures posing on the left
appear to be the guard and three intrepid passengers. Two tanks
of water sent from Ladmanlow stand on the ramp above the
engine.

The Hoffman lime kiln at Harpur with its siding, October 1950. It was demolished in 1952, having burned continuously since it was first lit in 1875.

below:
Test run of a B.T.H. Class 15 16-cylinder diesel electric locomotive ascending Hudlow Bank, December 9, 1958.

A Clay Cross Company train from Grin Works, Buxton, being
propelled to Ladmanlow by their vertical boilered sentinel 0–4–0
tank engine.

The Gloucestershire Railway Society Excursion of May 21, 1955 at Ladmanlow, which was the terminus of the line in 1892. In the background are the mountainous spoil heaps from the old Grin Quarries, now reclaimed and landscaped.

The S.L.S. and M.L.S. Railtour, June 27, 1953. The train is approaching Ladmanlow behind Midland 0–6–0, B.R. No. 43387.

The disused siding to the Clay Cross Company's Grin Limeworks is on the left of the main line.

Ladmanlow yard looking towards Whaley Bridge, July 6, 1932.

Hurdlow Station 1931. A train of six-wheeled carriages for Ashbourne is standing at the station behind a L.N.W.R. engine. Beyond the station, the former Hurdlow Incline can be seen climbing the hillside in spite of having been abandoned some 60 years previously.

The Whaley Bridge end of Burbage tunnel, July 9, 1932. The 5580 yard long tunnel was driven through the rock between Ladmanlow and Bunsall Top. It was abandoned on June 25, 1892 and the ends closed with wooden boarding, later to be bricked up.

It is of interest that sleeper-marks can be clearly discerned in the grass although they had been lifted 40 years before the photograph was taken.

L.M.S. Class 5f 0–8–4 Tank No. 7954 and Class 4f 0–6–0 No. 4382 snowed up at Briggs Siding, February 15, 1947. The engines had been stranded since February 4, and fires are being lit beneath them to thaw them out.

Bunsall Incline, July 9, 1932, showing on the left the site of the intermediate engine house. This was abandoned after June 8, 1857, when the two Inclines were combined into one.

inset: The crumbling remains of the winding engine house.

This is a view of the L.N.W.R. Manchester to Buxton line sometime in the nineteenth century. The C.H.P.R. passed beneath it at this point and a connecting line can be seen descending from the main line on the right-hand side together with some wagons standing on the approach to Whaley Bridge incline. Of especial interest is the 18th century beam engine and leadstocks in the centre. Subsidence from the old Shallcross Colliery Company workings caused a great deal of nuisance to the C.H.P.R. over a period of 20 years in this area.

Two wagons about to ascend Whaley Bridge Incline, July 9, 1932. This Incline climbed 180 yards on a gradient of 1 in 13½ and was used for the last time on April 9, 1952. On the left a siding leads into Goyt Mills.

The Peak Forest Canal at Whaley Bridge. The Cromford and High Peak Railway terminated to the left of the warehouses on the far side of the canal.